D1530519

American English Edition, published 2024 by National Geographic Partners, LLC., in association with HarperCollins Publishers Ltd.
Text copyright © 2024 HarperCollins Publishers. All Rights Reserved.
Design copyright © 2024 National Geographic Partners, LLC. All Rights Reserved.

NATIONAL GEOGRAPHIC and the Yellow Border Design are trademarks of the National Geographic Society, and used under license.

British English Edition, published 2019 by Collins, an imprint of HarperCollins Publishers Ltd., in association with National Geographic Partners, LLC.
Text copyright © 2018 HarperCollins Publishers. All Rights Reserved.
Design copyright © 2024 National Geographic Partners, LLC. All Rights Reserved.

All rights reserved. No part of this publication may be reproduced, stored in a retrieval system, or transmitted, in any form or by any means, electronic, mechanical, photocopying, recording, or otherwise without the prior permission in writing of the publisher and copyright owners.

ISBN: 978-1-4263-7143-1

The contents of this publication are believed correct at the time of printing. Nevertheless the publisher can accept no responsibility for errors or omissions, changes in the detail given, or for any expense or loss thereby caused.

Since 1888, the National Geographic Society has funded more than 14,000 research, conservation, education, and storytelling projects around the world. National Geographic Partners distributes a portion of the funds it receives from your purchase to the National Geographic Society to support programs including the conservation of animals and their habitats. To learn more, visit natgeo.com/info.

Printed in China
23/RRDH/1

Photo and Illustration Credits

AS: Adobe Stock; ASP: Alamy Stock Photo; SS: Shutterstock
Cover (Pterodactyl), Natalia Gorbach/SS; (Dimorphodon), AlienCat/AS; (Macrocollum), Franco Tempesta/© National Geographic Partners, LLC; (Coahuilaceratops), Franco Tempesta/© National Geographic Partners, LLC; (Apatosaurus), Warpaint/SS; (palm trees), Franco Tempesta/© National Geographic Partners, LLC; Spine (Macrocollum), Franco Tempesta/© National Geographic Partners, LLC; Back cover (LO), Herschel Hoffmeyer/SS; (UP), Sergey Krasovskiy/ASP; 1, Warpaint/SS; 3 (UP), Vac1/SS; 3 (RT), Warpaint/SS; 3 (LE), Herschel Hoffmeyer/SS; 4 (UP), Elenarts/SS; 4 (CTR), Warpaint/SS; 4 (LO), Michael Rosskothen/SS; 5 (UP), Herschel Hoffmeyer/SS; 5 (LO), Andreas Meyer/SS; 6, Catmando/SS; 8, Sergey Krasovskiy/Stocktrek Images/ASP; 9, Catmando/SS; 10, Herschel Hoffmeyer/SS; 11, Mineo/AS; 12-13, Friedrich Saurer/ASP; 14 (UP LE & UP RT), Catmando/SS; 14 (CTR LE), Friedrich Saurer/ASP; 14 (CTR RT), Herschel Hoffmeyer/SS; 14 (LO LE), Elenarts/SS; 14 (LO RT), Mineo/AS; 15 (UP LE), Herschel Hoffmeyer/SS; 15 (UP RT), Elenarts/SS; 15 (CTR LE), Mineo/AS; 15 (CTR RT), Catmando/SS; 15 (LO LE), Friedrich Saurer/ASP; 15 (LO RT), Catmando/SS; 16, Warpaint/SS; 17, Franco Tempesta/© National Geographic Partners, LLC; 18, Elenarts/AS; 19, Elenarts/AS; 20, Catmando/SS; 21, Arthur Dorety/Stocktrek Images/ASP; 22, DM7/SS; 24, AlienCat/AS; 25, Catmando/SS; 26, warpaintcobra/AS; 27, photosvac/AS; 28-29, Herschel Hoffmeyer/SS; 29, DM7/AS; 30 (UP LE), Sergey Krasovskiy/ASP; 30 (UP RT), Nobumichi Tamura/Stocktrek Images/ASP; 30 (CTR LE), Herschel Hoffmeyer/SS; 30 (CTR RT), Michael Rosskothen/AS; 30 (LO LE), Suwat wongkham/SS; 30 (LO RT), photosvac/AS; 31 (UP LE), Michael Rosskothen/AS; 31 (UP RT), Herschel Hoffmeyer/SS; 31 (CTR LE), photosvac/AS; 31 (CTR RT), Suwat wongkham/SS; 31 (LO LE), Sergey Krasovskiy/ASP; 31 (LO RT), Nobumichi Tamura/Stocktrek Images/ASP; 32, Herschel Hoffmeyer/SS; 33, Warpaint/SS; 54, metha1819/SS; 35, metha1819/SS; 36, Sergey Krasovskiy/ASP; 37, Catmando/SS; 38, Catmando/SS; 40, Warpaint/SS; 41, Michael Rosskothen/SS; 42, Herschel Hoffmeyer/SS; 43, Sergey Krasovskiy/Stocktrek Images/ASP; 44, Nobumichi Tamura/Stocktrek Images/ASP; 45, Herschel Hoffmeyer/SS; 46 (UP LE), Catmando/SS; 46 (UP RT), AlienCat/AS; 46 (CTR LE), Herschel Hoffmeyer/SS; 46 (CTR RT), Herschel Hoffmeyer/SS; 46 (LO LE), Warpaint/SS; 46 (LO RT), DM7/SS; 47 (UP LE), Warpaint/SS; 47 (UP RT), Herschel Hoffmeyer/SS; 47 (CTR LE), AlienCat/AS; 47 (CTR RT), DM7/SS; 47 (LO LE), Herschel Hoffmeyer/SS; 47 (LO RT), Catmando/SS; 48, Warpaint/SS; 49, DM7/SS; 50, Michael Rosskothen/SS; 51, Michael Rosskothen/SS; 52, QBR/SS; 53, Warpaint/SS; 54-55, Warpaint/SS; 56, Warpaint/SS; 57, Herschel Hoffmeyer/SS; 58, Noiel/SS; 58-59, Herschel Hoffmeyer/SS; 60, Bjoern Wylezich/SS; 61, Ton Bangkeaw/SS; 62 (UP LE), Catmando/SS; 62 (UP RT), Herschel Hoffmeyer/SS; 62 (CTR LE), Herschel Hoffmeyer/SS; 62 (CTR RT), Warpaint/SS; 62 (LO LE), Catmando/SS; 62 (LO RT), Catmando/SS; 63 (UP LE), Catmando/SS; 63 (UP RT), Warpaint/SS; 63 (CTR LE), Catmando/SS; 63 (CTR RT), Herschel Hoffmeyer/SS; 63 (LO LE), Catmando/SS; 63 (LO RT), Herschel Hoffmeyer/SS; 64-65, Warpaint/SS; 66, Catmando/SS; 67, Catmando/SS; 68, GOLFX/SS; 69, Warpaint/SS; 70, Michael Rosskothen/SS; 72, Natalia Gorbach/SS; 73, Herschel Hoffmeyer/SS; 74, AlienCat/AS; 75, Vac1/SS; 76, Herschel Hoffmeyer/SS; 77, Warpaint/SS; 78, Warpaint/SS; 79, Freer/SS; 80, Elenarts/SS; 81, Elenarts/SS; 82, Catmando/SS; 83, Andreas Meyer/SS

PUZZLE
book of
DINOSAURS

Tons of **COOL**
ACTIVITIES
and **FUN FACTS**

NATIONAL GEOGRAPHIC
WASHINGTON, D.C.

CONTENTS

Think you've got what it takes to tackle these wild puzzles? Test your skills with fun crosswords, sudokus, and more! Need a little help? No worries, you'll find solutions in the back of the book.

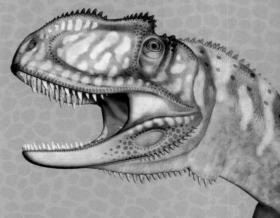

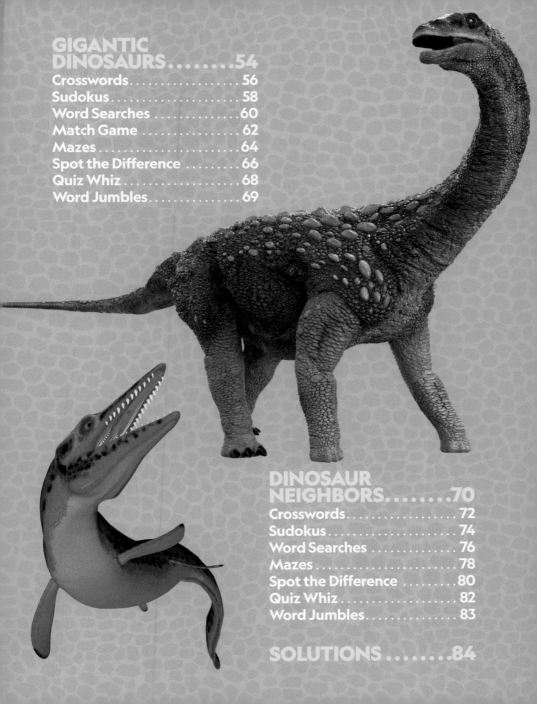

SMALL DINOSAURS

Get ready for **PUZZLES** and **FUN FACTS** about **SMALL DINOSAURS.**

OVIRAPTOR (OH-vih-RAP-tore) did not have teeth. This dinosaur used its **STRONG JAWS** to **CRUSH FOOD** such as lizards.

CROSSWORDS

Help this *Minmi* (MIN-mee) crack the crosswords by solving the cryptic clues below. The number of letters in each answer is shown in parentheses alongside the clue.

Can you guess the small dinosaur code words by using the letters in the colored squares?

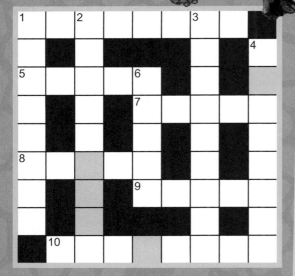

MINMI had a tough body that was covered in **HARD ARMOR.** Even its stomach skin had armor!

Across

1 Come close to (8)
5 Animal that eats bamboo (5)
7 Put your clothes on (5)
8 Famous deer (5)
9 Cooked slice of bread (5)
10 Animals that pull Santa's sleigh (8)

Down

1 The letters we use when writing (8)
2 To show by gestures and not talking (9)
3 To make an important day or event special (9)
4 Tragedy (8)
6 Reveal something to be true (5)

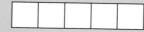

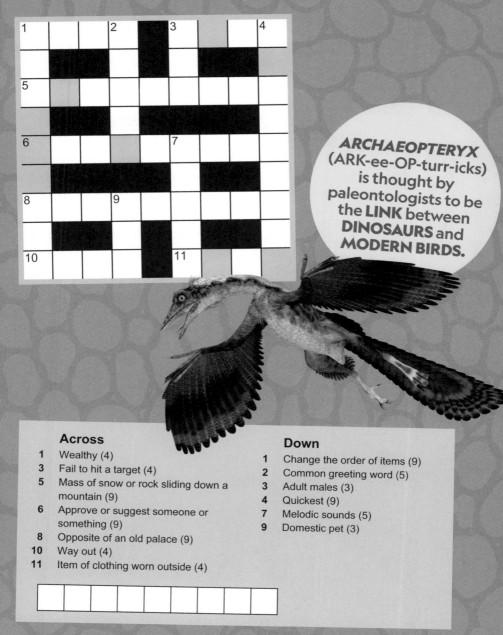

ARCHAEOPTERYX (ARK-ee-OP-turr-icks) is thought by paleontologists to be the **LINK** between **DINOSAURS** and **MODERN BIRDS.**

Across

1 Wealthy (4)
3 Fail to hit a target (4)
5 Mass of snow or rock sliding down a mountain (9)
6 Approve or suggest someone or something (9)
8 Opposite of an old palace (9)
10 Way out (4)
11 Item of clothing worn outside (4)

Down

1 Change the order of items (9)
2 Common greeting word (5)
3 Adult males (3)
4 Quickest (9)
7 Melodic sounds (5)
9 Domestic pet (3)

SUDOKUS

Solve the sudokus with help from this *Heterodontosaurus* (HET-er-oh-DON-toe-SORE-us).

Fill in the blank squares so that numbers 1 to 6 appear once in each row, column, and 3 × 2 box.

4	6			2	
1					4
	2				
				4	
3					2
	4			5	6

STRUTHIOMIMUS (strooth-ee-oh-MY-muss) was one of the **FASTEST RUNNERS** of all dinosaurs. Its legs were **LONG** and **STRONG**.

HETERODONTOSAURUS had **FIVE FINGERS.** Two of the fingers are thought to have been opposable, like thumbs, to help it grasp its **PREY.**

			3	6	
6	3				5
		4	5	1	
	5	1	6		
5				3	
	2	3	4		

		6		5	
2			4		
				1	3
3	1				
		4			1
	2		5		

WORD SEARCHES

This *Psittacosaurus* (SIT-ah-co-SORE-us) is on the lookout for its friends.

Search left to right and top to bottom to find the words listed in the boxes below.

u	h	o	t	o	m	b	s	p	b	w	m
l	e	f	y	w	i	a	i	o	u	i	i
l	r	f	h	s	c	g	l	c	i	t	c
s	b	r	m	f	r	a	u	u	t	e	r
t	i	y	i	v	o	c	o	l	r	i	o
r	v	q	n	g	c	e	s	s	e	s	r
d	o	w	m	e	e	r	a	a	r	g	a
q	r	j	i	u	r	a	u	j	a	k	p
t	e	u	a	d	a	t	r	r	p	o	t
a	y	c	l	l	t	o	u	l	t	i	o
j	a	f	q	l	u	p	s	u	o	i	r
q	a	n	t	a	s	s	a	u	r	u	s

bagaceratops	microraptor
buitreraptor	minmi
herbivore	qantassaurus
microceratus	siluosaurus

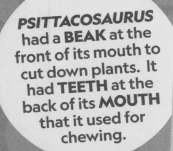

PSITTACOSAURUS had a **BEAK** at the front of its mouth to cut down plants. It had **TEETH** at the back of its **MOUTH** that it used for chewing.

l	d	i	r	p	z	y	u	s	w	e	d
i	o	x	i	x	i	a	n	y	k	u	s
a	l	j	t	i	o	e	k	u	r	l	s
o	v	i	r	a	p	t	o	r	w	c	i
c	l	t	a	t	i	s	a	u	r	u	s
e	o	r	a	p	t	o	r	m	r	y	e
r	s	a	l	n	h	r	b	e	a	c	v
a	q	q	u	b	u	t	f	i	s	l	u
t	d	r	a	c	o	p	e	l	t	a	t
o	w	e	k	r	a	u	v	o	q	w	s
p	a	z	c	t	g	l	j	n	t	s	u
s	o	f	a	n	j	r	n	g	u	i	l

claws

dracopelta

eoraptor

liaoceratops

mei long

oviraptor

tatisaurus

xixianykus

MATCH GAME

Match the magnified dinosaur parts to the dinosaur pictures on the next page.

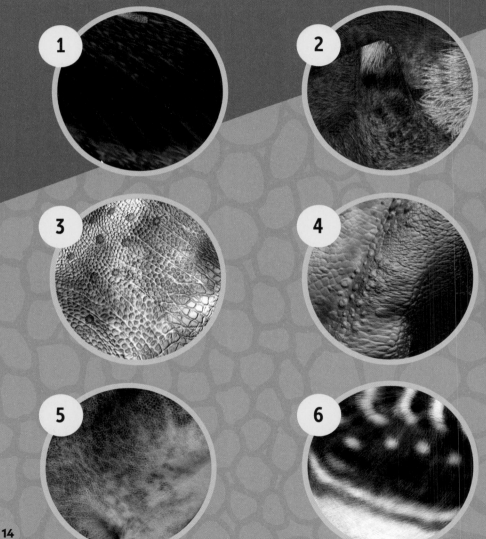

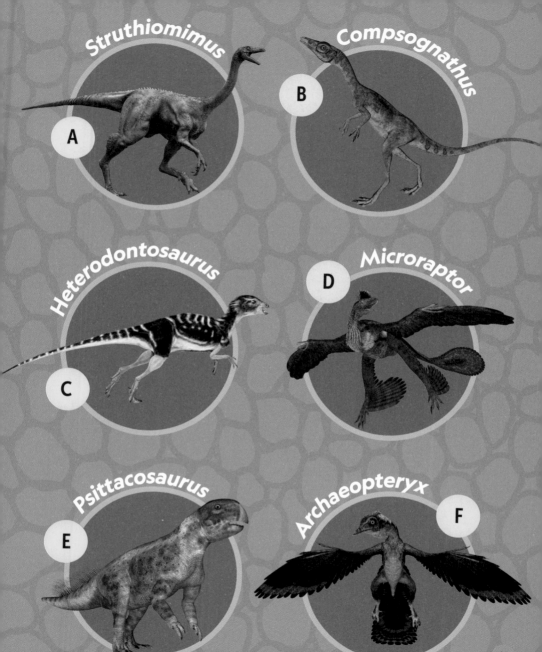

Struthiomimus

A

Compsognathus

B

Heterodontosaurus

C

Microraptor

D

Psittacosaurus

E

Archaeopteryx

F

15

MAZES

Lead this *Microraptor* (MY-crow-RAP-tore) through the mazes.

Work your way around the mazes until you reach the exit.

MICRORAPTOR weighed **UP TO TWO POUNDS (0.9 KG)!** It had feathers and wings, but **DID NOT FLY** like a bird. It could **GLIDE** through the air like a kite.

Some dinosaurs had **LONG, SHARP CLAWS** to **DEFEND** themselves from **PREDATORS.**

SPOT THE DIFFERENCE

Compare the two images of *Compsognathus* (KOMP-sog-NAH-thus).
Can you spot the five differences between the images?

COMPSOGNATHUS was one of the **SMALLEST** dinosaurs, but it used its size to its **ADVANTAGE**, relying on **SPEED** and **AGILITY** to **CATCH** prey.

QUIZ WHIZ

Can you guess the answers to the small dinosaur questions below?

1. *Microraptor* weighed about:
   a. 10 pounds (4.5 kg)
   b. 5 pounds (2.5 kg)
   c. 2 pounds (0.9 kg)

2. Which dinosaur's name means "ostrich mimic"?
   a. *Struthiomimus*
   b. *Scutellosaurus*
   c. *Minmi*

3. Dinosaurs that hunted other animals are called:
   a. Prey
   b. Predators
   c. Herbivores

4. *Oviraptor* had no:
   a. Arms
   b. Teeth
   c. Tail

5. How do scientists think *Leaellynasaura* kept warm?
   a. By building fires
   b. By wearing leaves
   c. By digging burrows

6. Which animals alive today are the closest relatives to dinosaurs?
   a. Birds
   b. Cats
   c. Horses

7. *Scutellosaurus*'s armor plates were the size of:
   a. Bottle tops
   b. Oak leaves
   c. Dinner plates

8. *Archaeopteryx* was a link between dinosaurs and:
   a. Insects
   b. Birds
   c. Crocodiles

9. *Huayangosaurus* had two large what over its hips?
   a. Wings
   b. Antennae
   c. Spikes

10. Scientists can tell what dinosaurs looked like by studying what?
    a. Photographs
    b. Fossils
    c. Recordings

COMPSOGNATHUS WAS ABOUT THE SIZE OF A **TURKEY.**

WORD JUMBLES

These *Buitreraptor* (BWEE-tre-RAP-tore) need help rearranging the jumbled letters to spell the names of other small dinosaurs.

R R I M O A T R O C P

N M I M I

A E I U B T R R T P O R

R P O V R I O T A

M S G A H S O U P T O N C

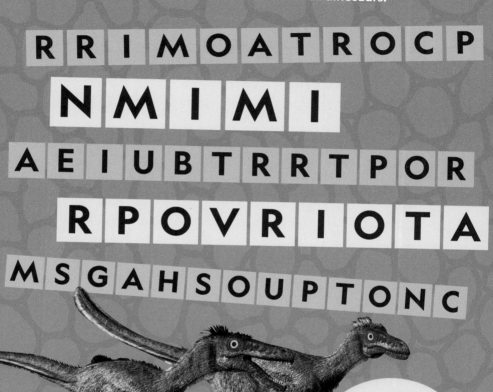

BUITRERAPTOR had very **SMALL TEETH**, which it used for hunting insects, lizards, and other animals.

BIG
DINOSAURS

Go back in time to discover **FUN FACTS** and play **PUZZLES** with **BIG DINOSAURS.**

CARNOTAURUS
(KAR-no-TORE-us) was a **STRANGE** dinosaur with a **SQUARISH HEAD,** **HORNS** like a bull, and eyes that faced forward. Its tiny arms were even shorter than **TYRANNOSAURUS'S** (tye-RAN-oh-SORE-us-ses).

CROSSWORDS

Help this *Corythosaurus* (co-RITH-oh-SORE-us) crack the crosswords by solving the cryptic clues below. The number of letters in each answer is shown in parentheses alongside the clue.

Can you guess the big dinosaur code words by using the letters in the colored squares?

When **CORYTHOSAURUS BREATHED** in, the air would travel from its **NOSE** up through the **CREST** on its **HEAD**. This may have made the dinosaur **SOUND LOUDER.**

Across
4   Common bird (6)
6   Otherwise (4)
7   A chicken might lay one (3)
8   Move through water (4)
9   Female relative (4)
10 Flying mammal (3)
11 Without cost or payment (4)
12 Show (6)

Down
1   You can see these in the sky on the Fourth of July (9)
2   Last month of the year (8)
3   Absolutely necessary (9)
5   Opposite of positive (8)

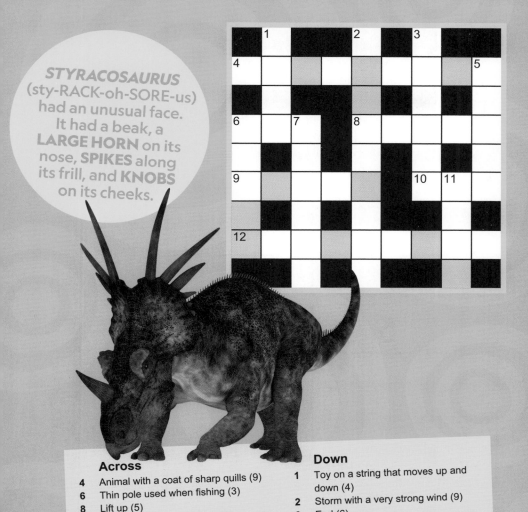

STYRACOSAURUS (sty-RACK-oh-SORE-us) had an unusual face. It had a beak, a **LARGE HORN** on its nose, **SPIKES** along its frill, and **KNOBS** on its cheeks.

Across

4 Animal with a coat of sharp quills (9)
6 Thin pole used when fishing (3)
8 Lift up (5)
9 Very simple (5)
10 Warm (3)
12 Very large hairy spider (9)

Down

1 Toy on a string that moves up and down (4)
2 Storm with a very strong wind (9)
3 End (6)
5 A thing that takes place (5)
6 Machine that may look like a human being (5)
7 A dry and often sandy region (6)
11 Birds of prey that hoot (4)

SUDOKUS

Solve the sudokus with help from this *Stegosaurus* (STEG-oh-SORE-us).

Fill in the blank squares so that numbers 1 to 6 appear once in each row, column, and 3 × 2 box.

	6			1	
	2	1	3		
					3
	5				
		2	6	5	
	1			4	

STEGOSAURUS had **HUGE SPIKES** on its tail, which it would use as a **WEAPON.** It would swing its big tail and smack its **ENEMY** with the spikes.

		2			5
			6	2	
4	1		2		
		3		1	6
	5	4			
3				4	

CRYOLOPHOSAURUS (CRY-oh-LOW-foh-SORE-us) was one of the **FIRST DINOSAURS** to be discovered on the continent of **ANTARCTICA.**

		6		3	
4		3			
2	4				
				4	1
			4		3
	5		6		

WORD SEARCHES

This *Ouranosaurus* (oo-RAHN-oh-SORE-us) is on the lookout for its friends.

Search left to right and top to bottom to find the words listed in the boxes below.

```
w  p  w  q  u  s  r  d  k  v  n  y
m  l  i  o  x  a  l  a  i  a  i  n
p  a  v  t  y  f  h  a  p  k  y  h
n  t  r  i  c  e  r  a  t  o  p  s
d  e  i  n  o  c  h  e  i  r  u  s
n  o  t  h  r  o  n  y  c  h  u  s
e  s  w  c  a  k  e  a  a  i  s  p
g  a  g  o  b  i  s  a  u  r  u  s
h  u  t  a  h  r  a  p  t  o  r  k
s  r  u  l  b  a  a  y  b  u  d  a
e  u  r  o  p  a  s  a  u  r  u  s
l  s  l  b  r  h  f  r  e  u  p  e
```

OURANOSAURUS lived in **RIVER** deltas and lowland flood-plains. When these areas flooded, **GIGANTIC CROCODILES** were a threat.

deinocheirus	oxalaia
europasaurus	plateosaurus
gobisaurus	triceratops
nothronychus	utahraptor

i	o	j	o	c	e	r	a	t	o	p	s
u	s	r	t	t	a	r	c	h	i	a	e
o	u	r	a	n	o	s	a	u	r	u	s
l	k	t	a	k	r	r	r	c	w	e	u
n	d	h	f	i	o	s	n	e	i	b	c
z	h	e	r	b	i	v	o	r	e	s	h
o	s	a	v	l	p	l	t	o	s	c	o
g	q	r	d	w	u	e	a	n	l	q	m
s	t	e	g	o	s	a	u	r	u	s	i
v	u	r	e	e	u	q	r	z	s	i	m
l	a	l	l	o	s	a	u	r	u	s	u
a	o	i	q	s	c	q	s	p	l	r	s

allosaurus

carnotaurus

herbivores

ojoceratops

ouranosaurus

stegosaurus

suchomimus

tarchia

More than **100 SKELETONS** of *PLATEOSAURUS* (PLAT-ee-oh-SORE-us) have been **FOUND** across **EUROPE.**

29

MATCH GAME

Match the magnified dinosaur parts to the dinosaur pictures on the next page.

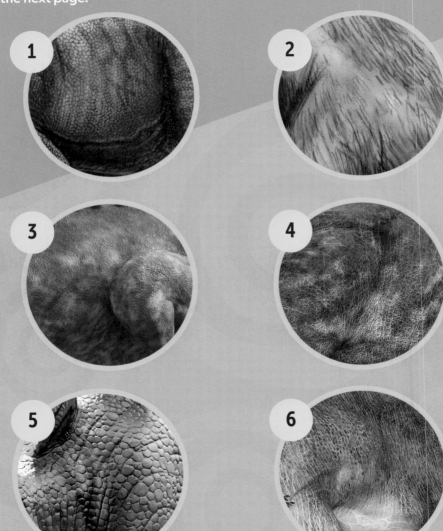

A Pentaceratops

B Pachycephalosaurus

C Utahraptor

D Stegosaurus

Herrerasaurus **E**

Nothronychus **F**

MAZES

Lead this *Utahraptor* (YOO-tah-RAP-tore) through the mazes.
Work your way around the mazes until you reach the exit.

UTAHRAPTOR
had **SCARY FEET!**
When **ATTACKING**
its prey, it would
KICK HARD and
STAB it with its **BIG
SHARP CLAWS.**

SPOT THE DIFFERENCE

Compare the two images of *Triceratops* (tri-SERR-uh-tops).
Can you spot the five differences between the images?

TRICERATOPS might have used its **HORNS** to **FIGHT OFF LARGER DINOSAURS.** A *Triceratops* fossil found in 1997 shows **PUNCTURE MARKS** that match the **BITE OF TYRANNOSAURUS.**

QUIZ WHIZ

Do you know the answers to the big dinosaur questions below?

1. How many horns did *Triceratops* have?
   a. 5
   b. 3
   c. 1

2. How many skeletons of *Plateosaurus* have been found?
   a. Ten
   b. Hundreds
   c. Thousands

3. *Ouranosaurus* lived in places where it was:
   a. Snowy
   b. Dry
   c. Wet

4. *Europasaurus* fossils were found in which European country?
   a. Germany
   b. England
   c. France

5. What do we call scientists that study dinosaurs?
   a. Dinotologists
   b. Fossilologists
   c. Paleontologists

6. *Stegosaurus*'s body was covered with what?
   a. Fur
   b. Fins
   c. Spikes

7. Which dinosaur's name means "meat-eating bull lizard"?
   a. *Carnotaurus*
   b. *Allosaurus*
   c. *Giganotosaurus*

8. *Muttaburrasaurus* was found on which continent?
   a. North America
   b. Australia
   c. Asia

9. Dinosaurs that ate only plants are called?
   a. Saladivores
   b. Vegivores
   c. Herbivores

10. Which insect was alive when dinosaurs were?
    a. Dragonfly
    b. Butterfly
    c. Ladybird

HERRERASAURUS
(huh-RARE-ah-SORE-us)
was one of the earliest
MEAT-EATING DINOSAURS.

WORD JUMBLES

This *Europasaurus* (yoo-ROPE-ah-SORE-us) needs help rearranging the jumbled letters to spell the names of big dinosaurs.

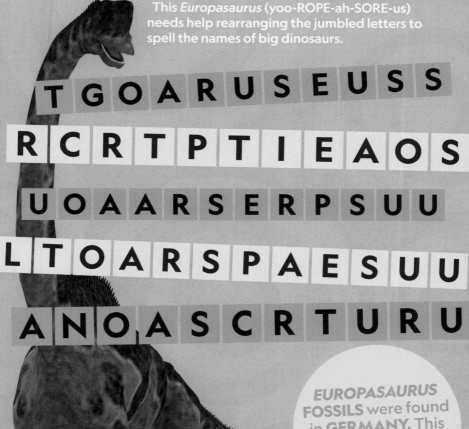

TGOARUSEUSS

RCRTPTIEAOS

UOAARSERPSUU

LTOARSPAESUU

ANOASCRTURU

EUROPASAURUS FOSSILS were found in GERMANY. This dinosaur LIVED IN FORESTS on islands.

GIANT DINOSAURS

Keep a lookout for PUZZLES and FUN FACTS about GIANT DINOSAURS!

ANKYLOSAURUS (AN-kye-loh-SORE-us) moved very SLOWLY but would not run away from a FIGHT. Its full body was covered in ARMOR, and it had a HARD, BONY CLUB at the end of its TAIL.

39

CROSSWORDS

Help this *Iguanodon* (ih-GWAN-uh-don) crack the crosswords by solving the cryptic clues below. The number of letters in each answer is shown in parentheses alongside the clue.

Can you guess the giant dinosaur code words by using the letters in the colored squares?

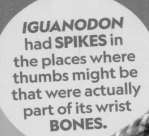

IGUANODON had **SPIKES** in the places where thumbs might be that were actually part of its wrist **BONES.**

Across

4 Run very quickly (6)
6 Danger; peril (4)
7 Seize (4)
8 Thought or suggestion (4)
9 Anagram of "now" (3)
10 Hot molten rock from a volcano (4)
11 Thanksgiving bird (6)

Down

1 Written in capital letters (9)
2 Rescue vehicle used on water (8)
3 Unexplained things (9)
5 Fitness instructors (8)

Across

4. Say no to (6)
6. Tidy (4)
7. Area of mown grass in a garden (4)
8. School test (4)
9. Slippery snakelike fish (3)
10. Camera part (4)
11. Evening meal (6)

Down

1. Constant; lasting indefinitely (9)
2. Commercial activity (8)
3. Person in a story (9)
5. Paper cover for a letter (8)

BIG TEETH and BIG CLAWS made YANGCHUANOSAURUS (YANG-chew-an-oh-SORE-us) a FIERCE PREDATOR. It could KILL prey MUCH BIGGER than itself.

41

SUDOKUS

Solve the sudokus with help from this *Acrocanthosaurus* (ACK-row-CAN-tho-SORE-us).

Fill in the blank squares so that the numbers 1 to 6 appear once in each row, column, and 3 × 2 box.

			6	1	
		4		2	
		5		6	
	6		5		
	5		4		
	4	3			

ACROCANTHOSAURUS had **38 SHARP TEETH** in its **UPPER JAW.** It was **ONE OF THE BIGGEST MEAT-EATING DINOSAURS.**

Grid 1

		3	1		
	1				
	2	5		4	
	4		5	1	
				5	
		4	6		

TSINTAOSAURUS (sin-tau-SORE-us) had a long crest that grew out of its forehead, making it look like the MYTHICAL UNICORN.

Grid 2

6					
		2		6	
	6	3	5		
		5	2	3	
	1		6		
					5

43

WORD SEARCHES

This *Amargasaurus* (uh-MARG-uh-SORE-us) is on the lookout for its friends.

Search left to right and top to bottom to find the words listed in the boxes below.

m	a	i	a	s	a	u	r	a	a	m	a
s	z	j	n	x	a	r	g	i	f	a	m
a	a	q	k	a	r	i	u	e	a	p	a
u	a	k	y	c	i	o	l	a	l	u	r
r	e	b	l	e	r	j	m	i	p	s	g
o	a	r	o	j	t	a	j	n	a	a	a
l	e	s	s	e	m	s	a	u	r	u	s
o	m	x	a	r	z	a	l	t	o	r	a
p	l	e	u	r	a	u	r	c	a	u	u
h	l	t	r	j	t	r	s	p	r	s	r
u	s	s	u	y	a	u	h	t	j	i	u
s	l	a	s	d	w	s	i	c	f	l	s

AMARGASAURUS had a **LONG NECK** with a **DOUBLE ROW** of **SPINES**.

amargasaurus
ankylosaurus
lessemsaurus
maiasaura

mapusaurus
riojasaurus
roar
saurolophus

s	x	d	s	a	b	o	n	e	s	t	u
m	f	o	s	s	i	l	s	m	p	i	m
p	o	r	c	x	g	a	r	a	i	t	v
s	l	r	i	i	u	j	u	g	n	a	s
k	i	m	r	c	a	u	o	n	o	n	t
w	h	y	c	o	n	r	o	a	s	o	f
g	l	t	t	l	o	a	m	p	a	s	u
h	e	l	q	d	d	s	w	a	u	a	t
c	s	h	u	n	o	s	a	u	r	u	s
l	h	p	l	y	n	i	i	l	u	r	o
l	q	u	s	q	e	c	u	i	s	i	k
j	s	z	t	r	t	i	s	a	q	t	z

bones
fossils
iguanodon
jurassic

magnapaulia
shunosaurus
spinosaurus
titanosaur

THERIZINOSAURUS
(THERE-ih-ZIN-oh-SORE-us)
had **HUGE CLAWS** that were
**ABOUT THREE FEET
(1 M) LONG!**

MATCH GAME

Match the magnified dinosaur parts to the dinosaur pictures on the next page.

Tyrannosaurus

A

Therizinosaurus

B

Ankylosaurus

C

Yangchuanosaurus

D

Spinosaurus

E

Maiasaura

F

MAZES

Lead this *Edmontosaurus* (ed-MON-toh-SORE-us) through the mazes.

Work your way around the mazes until you reach the exit.

EDMONTOSAURUS **TRAVELED** far and wide to **FIND FOOD.** The dinosaurs moved in herds and **WALKED MANY MILES** every year.

TYRANNOSAURUS is one of the most **FAMOUS DINOSAURS.** It was a **FEROCIOUS HUNTER** that could have **SWALLOWED** some small dinosaurs **WITHOUT CHEWING!**

SPOT THE DIFFERENCE

Compare the two images of *Spinosaurus* (SPINE-oh-SORE-us).
Can you spot the five differences between the images?

While other prehistoric creatures lived in water, **SPINOSAURUS** is the **ONLY KNOWN SEMIAQUATIC DINOSAUR.**

QUIZ WHIZ

Can you guess the answers to the giant dinosaur questions below?

1. *Tyrannosaurus*'s teeth were the same size as which fruit?
   a. Apples
   b. Bananas
   c. Pineapples

2. Which dinosaur had a crest that looked like the horn of a unicorn?
   a. *Tsintaosaurus*
   b. *Uniraptor*
   c. *Deinocheirus*

3. All dinosaurs did what?
   a. Walked on four legs
   b. Ate meat
   c. Laid eggs

4. *Shunosaurus* had what at the end of its tail?
   a. Feather fan
   b. Bony lump
   c. Sharp fork

5. *Therizinosaurus*'s claws were about how long?
   a. 3 feet (1 m)
   b. 10 feet (3 m)
   c. 3 inches (7.5 cm)

6. *Edmontosaurus*'s teeth were shaped like what?
   a. Hearts
   b. Diamonds
   c. Squares

7. What happened to the first *Spinosaurus* bones found?
   a. They were lost at sea.
   b. They were stolen.
   c. They were blown up.

8. Meat-eating dinosaur eggs were what shape?
   a. Big and round
   b. Long and thin
   c. Short and fat

9. *Maiasaura* used what to keep its eggs warm?
   a. Rotting vegetation
   b. Feathers
   c. Body heat

10. *Ankylosaurus* used which of these for protection?
    a. Spikes
    b. Armor
    c. Shell

SPINOSAURUS had a **LONG JAW** like a **CROCODILE'S**. It caught **FISH** to eat.

WORD JUMBLES

This *Shunosaurus* (SHOO-noh-SORE-us) needs help rearranging the jumbled letters to spell the names of giant dinosaurs.

R Y A N A S U T O S U R N

G A O O I U N D N

P N S U U S I O A R S

A A A R M I S U A

H N S U U S U O A R S

SHUNOSAURUS had a **LONG TAIL** with a bony lump on the end. It could **SWING ITS TAIL** and **HIT ENEMIES** with the hard end, which also **HAD AT LEAST TWO SPIKES!**

GIGANTIC DINOSAURS

Watch out for PUZZLES and FUN FACTS about GIGANTIC DINOSAURS!

DIPLODOCUS'S TAIL (dih-PLOD-uh-kus-ses) was **LONGER** than any other dinosaur's. Its **TAIL** had up to **80 VERTEBRAE.**

CROSSWORDS

Help this *Apatosaurus* (uh-PAT-uh-SORE-us) crack the crosswords by solving the cryptic clues below. The number of letters in each answer is shown in parentheses alongside the clue.

Can you guess the gigantic dinosaur code words by using the letters in the colored squares?

Across

4 At the back of (6)
6 You use these to hear (4)
7 Opposite of minus (4)
8 Marine crustacean that has pincers (4)
9 One plus one equals (3)
10 No person (6)

Down

1 Baby eagle (6)
2 Opposite of multiplication (8)
3 You might spread this on toast (9)
5 Give details about (8)

APATOSAURUS traveled in herds. The dinosaurs may have **PROTECTED THEIR YOUNG** by keeping them in the **MIDDLE** of the group.

SALTASAURUS (SALT-ah-SORE-us) had **ARMORED PLATES**, similar to **CROCODILES'**, in its **SKIN**.

Across

4 Pieces of jewelry (9)
6 Form of public transportation (3)
8 Shout of encouragement (5)
9 Let happen (5)
10 Attempt (3)
12 Extinct animals that were often huge (9)

Down

1 List of food items at a restaurant (4)
2 The direction the hands on a watch move (9)
3 The way a person speaks that shows where they are from (6)
5 Feeling regret (5)
6 Get on an airplane (5)
7 Saying nothing (6)
11 Unusual or uncommon (4)

SUDOKUS

Solve the sudokus with help from this *Alamosaurus* (AL-uh-moe-SORE-us).

Fill in the blank squares so that the numbers 1 to 6 appear once in each row, column, and 3 × 2 box.

		5		3	
	3		4		
	1		5		
		4		1	
		1		5	
	2		3		

Long ago, a **PALEONTOLOGIST** thought he had discovered a new dinosaur and called it **BRONTOSAURUS** (BRON-toh-SORE-us). Years later, the **FOSSILS** were **FOUND** to actually be **APATOSAURUS** fossils!

Puzzle 1

			6		
1	4	6			
	2				5
4				2	
			5	3	2
		3			

Puzzle 2

	5		2	6	
2					
	1	4			
			3	4	
					6
	2	5		3	

ALAMOSAURUS was named after **OJO ALAMO,** a **SANDSTONE** formation in **NEW MEXICO, U.S.A.**

WORD SEARCHES

This *Brachiosaurus* (BRACK-ee-oh-SORE-us) is on the lookout for its friends.

Search left to right and top to bottom to find the words listed in the boxes below.

r	p	a	t	a	g	o	t	i	t	a	n
n	a	c	e	r	a	n	n	l	p	x	o
c	n	f	y	o	e	x	t	i	n	c	t
e	g	m	e	k	x	u	m	z	m	o	o
a	a	l	s	k	s	j	r	r	o	b	c
s	e	a	u	v	p	l	s	t	t	m	o
o	a	i	u	o	g	n	x	v	l	u	l
o	t	l	c	y	n	s	e	s	t	s	o
w	k	c	a	r	n	i	v	o	r	e	s
a	i	d	i	p	l	o	d	o	c	u	s
u	i	p	r	s	t	h	u	a	t	m	u
b	r	o	n	t	o	s	a	u	r	u	s

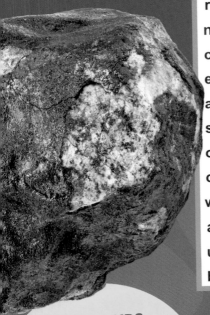

DINOSAURS DISAPPEARED around 65 MILLION YEARS AGO. Scientists think a BIG ASTEROID HIT EARTH, making it colder, which KILLED ALMOST ALL THE DINOSAURS.

brontosaurus
carnivores
diplodocus
extinct

museum
notocolossus
pangaea
patagotitan

p	s	a	u	r	o	p	o	d	s	t	l
a	l	a	m	o	s	a	u	r	u	s	v
r	l	o	b	j	z	z	a	p	p	p	i
a	s	t	e	r	o	i	d	p	e	q	v
l	a	p	a	t	o	s	a	u	r	u	s
i	e	p	a	k	l	q	d	l	s	u	o
t	g	p	y	a	j	j	d	l	a	o	t
i	n	u	r	o	s	a	u	r	u	s	x
t	o	e	s	a	g	a	z	p	r	e	c
a	s	x	s	u	e	w	w	u	u	o	a
n	s	m	g	u	o	t	v	l	s	v	t
r	s	k	h	r	b	o	z	l	c	a	n

alamosaurus
apatosaurus
asteroid
nurosaurus

paralititan
sauropods
supersaurus
toes

BRACHIOSAURUS had a very **LONG NECK,** and its front legs were longer than its back legs. **THIS HELPED** it **REACH THE LEAVES** of **TALL TREES.**

MATCH GAME

Match the magnified dinosaur parts to the dinosaur pictures on the next page.

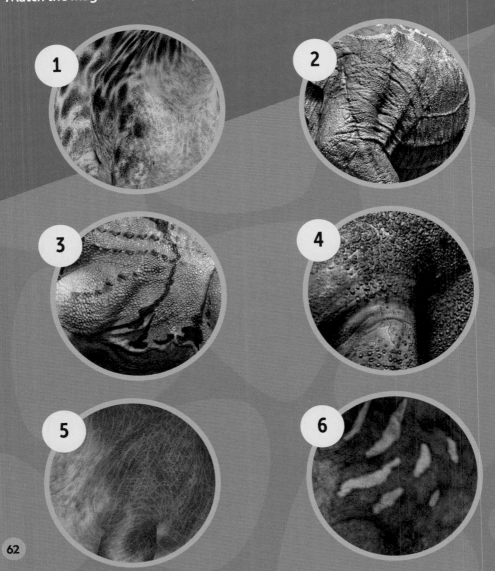

1

2

3

4

5

6

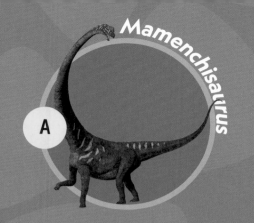

Mamenchisaurus

A

Saltasaurus

B

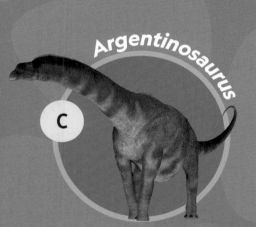

Argentinosaurus

C

Apatosaurus

D

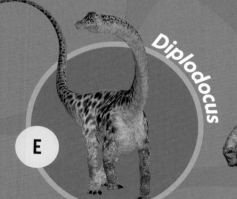

Diplodocus

E

Alamosaurus

F

MAZES

Lead this *Argentinosaurus* (ahr-gen-TEEN-oh-SORE-us) through the mazes.

Work your way around the mazes until you reach the exit.

ARGENTINOSAURUS was the **BIGGEST KNOWN ANIMAL** that **EVER LIVED** on land!

SPOT THE DIFFERENCE

Compare the two images of *Diplodocus* (dih-PLOD-uh-kus).
Can you spot the five differences between the images?

One of the **MOST FAMOUS** replicas of a **DIPLODOCUS** skeleton is **DIPPY,** housed in the entrance hall of **LONDON'S NATURAL HISTORY MUSEUM.**

QUIZ WHIZ

Can you guess the answers to the gigantic dinosaur questions below?

1. *Brontosaurus* fossils actually came from which dinosaur?
   a. *Tyrannosaurus*
   b. *Apatosaurus*
   c. *Triceratops*

2. Gigantic dinosaurs had brains the size of:
   a. Two chicken eggs
   b. A coconut
   c. Three tennis balls

3. *Paralititan* weighed up to:
   a. 3,000 tons (2,700 t)
   b. 80 tons (70 t)
   c. 100 tons (90 t)

4. Where can you still find araucarian trees that *Argentinosaurus* might have eaten?
   a. Brazil
   b. Scotland
   c. Argentina

5. *Diplodocus*'s tail stretched more than:
   a. 21 feet (6 m)
   b. 24 feet (7 m)
   c. 30 feet (9 m)

6. The oldest *Rebbachisaurus* fossil was found in:
   a. Morocco
   b. Singapore
   c. Canada

7. *Mamenchisaurus* bones were discovered in China by:
   a. Teachers
   b. Police officers
   c. Builders

8. Woolly mammoths were not dinosaurs because they had:
   a. Gills
   b. Fur
   c. Scales

9. Most dinosaurs walked on their:
   a. Back legs
   b. Hands
   c. Toes

10. Where can you go to look at dinosaur bones and fossils?
    a. Museums
    b. Hospitals
    c. Supermarkets

BIG OR SMALL, scaly or feathery—most **DINOSAURS WALKED** on their **TOES!**

WORD JUMBLES

This *Mamenchisaurus* (mah-MEHN-chee-SORE-us) needs help rearranging the jumbled letters to spell the names of gigantic dinosaurs.

I L D C S D P O O U

R N O A R S B O T S U U

R C I S U U B A H O A R S

A E C I A R S M M N H S U U

R G N N O U S U R E A I T A S

MAMENCHISAURUS DIDN'T USE its **LONG NECK** to **REACH HIGH INTO TREES.** Its neck was held **HORIZONTALLY** and may have allowed it to **REACH LOW SWAMP VEGETATION** from dry land.

DINOSAUR NEIGHBORS

Explore **FUN FACTS** and **PUZZLES** about **DINOSAUR NEIGHBORS** in this chapter!

ICHTHYOSAURUS (ICK-thee-oh-SORE-us) may have looked like a dolphin, but it was actually a **MARINE REPTILE.** Scientists think that its **LARGE EAR BONES** were used for **FINDING FISH** in the water or listening for **PREDATORS.**

CROSSWORDS

Help this *Pterodactylus* (ter-uh-DAK-til-us) crack the crosswords by solving the cryptic clues below. The number of letters in each answer is shown in parentheses alongside the clue.

Can you guess the dinosaur neighbor code words by using the letters in the colored squares?

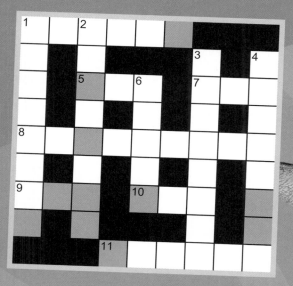

The name *PTERODACTYLUS* comes from Greek words meaning **"WINGED FINGER."** Pterodactyls had very long, specially adapted **FOURTH FINGERS.**

Across

1   Frightened (6)
5   Nine plus one (3)
7   Goal or purpose (3)
8   Large reptile similar to a crocodile (9)
9   Jump on one leg (3)
10 Item of neckwear often worn with a suit (3)
11 Dried grape (6)

Down

1   Feeling of sorrow for another (8)
2   Wild deerlike animal (8)
3   Soft part of a bed (8)
4   Person from the U.S.A. (8)
6   Opposite of day (5)

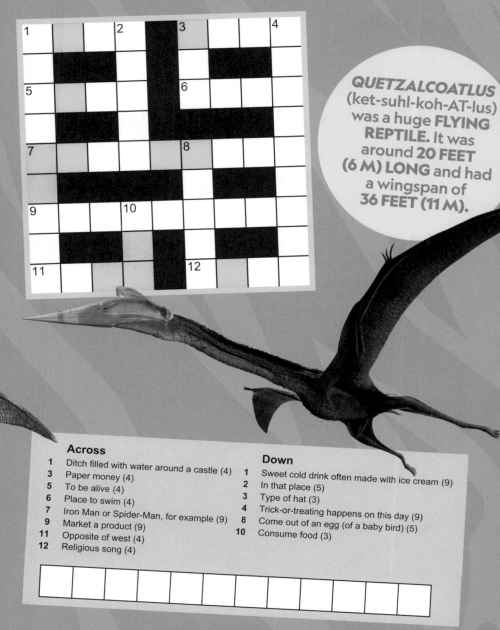

QUETZALCOATLUS (ket-suhl-koh-AT-lus) was a huge **FLYING REPTILE.** It was around **20 FEET (6 M) LONG** and had a wingspan of **36 FEET (11 M).**

Across

1 Ditch filled with water around a castle (4)
3 Paper money (4)
5 To be alive (4)
6 Place to swim (4)
7 Iron Man or Spider-Man, for example (9)
9 Market a product (9)
11 Opposite of west (4)
12 Religious song (4)

Down

1 Sweet cold drink often made with ice cream (9)
2 In that place (5)
3 Type of hat (3)
4 Trick-or-treating happens on this day (9)
8 Come out of an egg (of a baby bird) (5)
10 Consume food (3)

73

SUDOKUS

Solve the sudokus with help from this *Dimorphodon* (dye-MORPH-o-don).

Fill in the blank squares so that the numbers 1 to 6 appear once in each row, column, and 3 × 2 box.

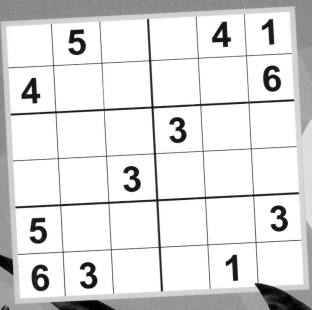

> **DIMORPHODON** had a **LONG TAIL** with a **DIAMOND-SHAPED FLAP** of skin on the end. This may have **HELPED IT STAY STEADY** as it glided through the **AIR.**

PTERANODON (ter-RAN-oh-don) was a **FLYING REPTILE** that lived at the same time as dinosaurs. **ITS WINGS** were as long as **25 FEET (8 M).** That's as large as a **HANG GLIDER!**

WORD SEARCHES

This *Kronosaurus* (CROW-no-SORE-us) is on the lookout for its friends.

Search left to right and top to bottom to find the words listed in the boxes below.

p	t	e	r	o	d	a	c	t	y	l	o
v	z	e	u	p	a	r	k	e	r	i	a
v	q	w	t	i	r	c	a	m	r	o	b
v	a	y	t	d	s	h	r	d	j	p	x
r	o	n	h	t	o	o	l	y	z	l	l
m	e	f	l	o	r	s	p	s	e	e	z
g	q	v	d	d	h	a	h	p	r	u	k
p	l	i	o	s	a	u	r	u	s	r	u
b	r	m	f	c	j	r	d	p	s	o	r
m	o	s	a	s	a	u	r	x	w	d	b
p	l	e	s	i	o	s	a	u	r	o	d
e	p	t	e	r	a	n	o	d	o	n	e

KRONOSAURUS is believed to have used its **POWERFUL JAWS** to shake and crush its prey.

archosaurus
euparkeria
liopleurodon
mosasaur

plesiosaur
pliosaurus
pteranodon
pterodactyl

p	a	r	a	s	u	c	h	u	s	m	p
m	o	l	a	d	w	t	u	n	r	b	o
o	d	l	l	i	k	g	c	v	q	n	s
v	b	m	i	m	i	d	s	i	t	a	t
n	o	t	h	o	s	a	u	r	c	l	o
i	z	u	k	r	s	q	s	s	d	o	s
e	a	b	e	p	t	s	f	p	s	f	u
i	c	h	t	h	y	o	s	a	u	r	c
s	a	r	c	o	s	u	c	h	u	s	h
g	g	u	l	d	c	o	l	s	t	m	u
u	u	h	a	o	p	t	e	r	u	s	s
l	k	r	o	n	o	s	a	u	r	u	s

POSTOSUCHUS
(POST-oh-SOOK-us)
might have been able
to **REAR UP** on its
HIND LEGS to **LUNGE**
AT ITS PREY.

dimorphodon
haopterus
ichthyosaur
kronosaurus

nothosaur
parasuchus
postosuchus
sarcosuchus

MAZES

Lead this *Liopleurodon* (LIE-oh-PLOOR-oh-don) through the mazes.

Work your way around the mazes until you reach the exit.

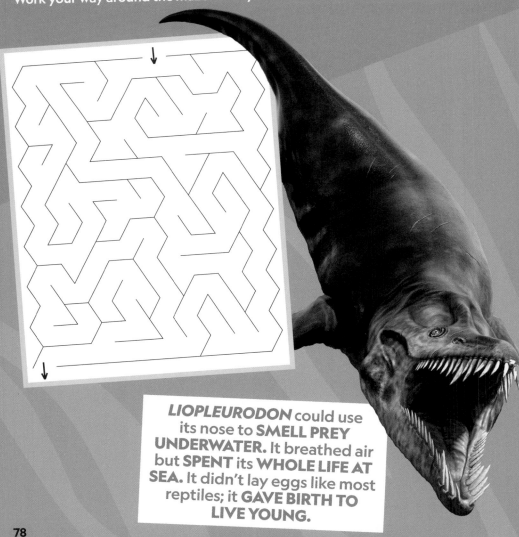

LIOPLEURODON could use its nose to **SMELL PREY UNDERWATER.** It breathed air but **SPENT** its **WHOLE LIFE AT SEA.** It didn't lay eggs like most reptiles; it **GAVE BIRTH TO LIVE YOUNG.**

PLESIOSAURUS
(PLEE-see-uh-SORE-us)
had a **LONG NECK,
SLEEK BODY,** small head,
and wide flippers. It is
believed it **ACTED VERY
MUCH LIKE** the **SEA
TURTLES** alive today.

SPOT THE DIFFERENCE

Compare the two images of *Pteranodon* (ter-RAN-oh-don).

Can you spot the five differences between the images?

The name **PTERANODON** comes from **GREEK** words meaning **"TOOTHLESS WING,"** as it **LACKED** the **SHARP TEETH** common to other members of its family.

QUIZ WHIZ

Can you guess the answers to the dinosaur neighbor questions below?

1. What was the shape of the skin flap on the end of *Dimorphodon*'s tail?
   a. Square
   b. Diamond
   c. Heart

2. Mosasaurs had two sets of:
   a. Teeth
   b. Eyes
   c. Wings

3. Ichthyosaurs liked to eat:
   a. Plants
   b. Insects
   c. Fish

4. *Kronosaurus* could grow up to:
   a. 16 feet (5 m)
   b. 26 feet (8 m)
   c. 33 feet (10 m)

5. *Megazostrodon* weighed as much as:
   a. A bowling ball
   b. An AA battery
   c. A pineapple

6. Pterodactyl wings were similar to which modern animal's wings?
   a. Butterfly
   b. Bat
   c. Hummingbird

7. *Sarcosuchus* lived in:
   a. North America
   b. Europe
   c. Africa

8. *Thrinaxodon* lived in:
   a. Burrows
   b. Nests
   c. Hives

9. *Pteranodon* had a wingspan of:
   a. 24 feet (7 m)
   b. 30 feet (9 m)
   c. 45 feet (14 m)

10. Pseudosuchia means:
   a. False cats
   b. False teeth
   c. False crocodiles

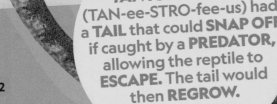

TANYSTROPHEUS (TAN-ee-STRO-fee-us) had a **TAIL** that could **SNAP OFF** if caught by a **PREDATOR**, allowing the reptile to **ESCAPE**. The tail would then **REGROW**.

WORD JUMBLES

This mosasaur (MOE-suh-sore) needs help rearranging the jumbled letters to spell the names of dinosaur neighbors.

S A O R S U M A S

R N A O N O D E T P

U I E A L S P U R S O S

R S N O O K R A U S U

U E L O I P R D N O O L

Similar to snakes, **MOSASAURS** had **JAWS** that could expand to **SWALLOW LARGE, WHOLE PREY.** They also had **TWO SETS OF TEETH** to help them **HOLD ON TO** struggling **PREY.**

SOLUTIONS

CROSWORDS 8-9

Code Word: *MINMI*

R	I	C	H		M	I	S	S
E		E			E			P
A	V	A	L	A	N	C	H	E
R		L			L			E
R	E	C	O	M	M	E	N	D
A					U			I
N	E	W	C	A	S	T	L	E
G		A			I			S
E	X	I	T		C	O	A	T

Code Word: *OVIRAPTOR*

SUDOKUS 10-11

4	6	5	1	2	3
1	3	2	5	6	4
5	2	4	6	3	1
6	1	3	2	4	5
3	5	6	4	1	2
2	4	1	3	5	6

4	1	5	3	6	2
6	3	2	1	4	5
2	6	4	5	1	3
3	5	1	6	2	4
5	4	6	2	3	1
1	2	3	4	5	6

4	3	6	1	5	2
2	5	1	4	3	6
6	4	5	2	1	3
3	1	2	6	4	5
5	6	4	3	2	1
1	2	3	5	6	4

WORD SEARCHES 12-13

MATCH GAME

14–15

1 – F *Archaeopteryx*
3 – E *Psittacosaurus*
5 – B *Compsognathus*

2 – D *Microraptor*
4 – A *Struthiomimus*
6 – C *Heterodontosaurus*

MAZES

16–17

SPOT THE DIFFERENCE

18–19

SOLUTIONS

QUIZ WHIZ 20

1. c – 2 pounds (0.9 kg)
2. a – *Struthiomimus*
3. b – Predators
4. b – Teeth
5. c – By digging burrows
6. a – Birds
7. a – Bottle tops
8. b – Birds
9. c – Spikes
10. b – Fossils

WORD JUMBLES 21

MICRORAPTOR
MINMI

BUITRERAPTOR
OVIRAPTOR

COMPSOGNATHUS

CROSSWORDS 24-25

Code Word: *TRICERATOPS*

Code Word: *CARNOTAURUS*

SUDOKUS 26-27

3	6	4	5	1	2
5	2	1	3	6	4
2	4	6	1	3	5
1	5	3	4	2	6
4	3	2	6	5	1
6	1	5	2	4	3

6	4	2	1	3	5
1	3	5	6	2	4
4	1	6	2	5	3
5	2	3	4	1	6
2	5	4	3	6	1
3	6	1	5	4	2

5	2	6	1	3	4
4	1	3	5	2	6
2	4	1	3	6	5
6	3	5	2	4	1
1	6	2	4	5	3
3	5	4	6	1	2

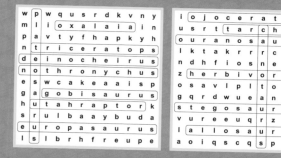

1 - E *Herrerasaurus*

3 - B *Pachycephalosaurus*

5 - D *Stegosaurus*

2 - F *Nothronychus*

4 - A *Pentaceratops*

6 - C *Utahraptor*

SOLUTIONS

SPOT THE DIFFERENCE   34–35

QUIZ WHIZ   36

1. b – 3
2. b – Hundreds
3. c – Wet
4. a – Germany
5. c – Paleontologists

6. c – Spikes
7. a – *Carnotaurus*
8. b – Australia
9. c – Herbivores
10. a – Dragonfly

WORD JUMBLES   37

STEGOSAURUS
TRICERATOPS

EUROPASAURUS
PLATEOSAURUS

CARNOTAURUS

Left crossword:
```
U  L        M
S P R I N T    M Y
  P  F    R I S K
  E  E    A   T
G R A B    I D E A
  C  O W N    R
L A V A    E   I
  S  T U R K E Y
  E          S   S
```
Code Word: *ANKYLOSAURUS*

Right crossword:
```
  P  B       C
R E F U S E    H
  R  S    N E A T
  M  I    V    R
L A W N    E X A M
  N  E E L    C
L E N S    O    T
  N  S U P P E R
  T          E   R
```
Code Word: *SPINOSAURUS*

```
5 3 2 6 1 4
6 1 4 3 2 5
4 2 5 1 6 3
3 6 1 5 4 2
2 5 6 4 3 1
1 4 3 2 5 6
```

```
4 6 3 1 2 5
5 1 2 4 6 3
1 2 5 3 4 6
3 4 6 5 1 2
6 3 1 2 5 4
2 5 4 6 3 1
```

```
6 3 1 4 5 2
4 5 2 3 6 1
2 6 3 5 1 4
1 4 5 2 3 6
5 1 4 6 2 3
3 2 6 1 4 5
```

```
m a i a s a u r a  a m a
s z j n x a r g i f  a m a
a a q k a r i u e a  p a r
u a k y c i o l a l  u r g
r e b l e r j m i p  s g a
o a r o j t a j n a  a a a
l e s s e m s a u r  u s
o m x a r z a l t o  r a
p l e u r a u r c a  u u
h l t r j t r s p r  s r
u s s u y a u h t j  i u
s l a s d w s i c f  l s
```

```
s x d s a b o n e s t u m
m f o s s i l s m p i u
p o r c x g a r a i t v
s l r i i u j u g n a s
k i m r c a u o n o n t
w h y c o n r o a s o f
g l t t l o a m p a s u
h e l q d d s w a u a t
c s h u n o s a u r u s
l h p l y n i i l u r o
l q u s q e c u i s i k
j s z t r t i s a q t z
```

SOLUTIONS

MATCH GAME   46–47

1 - F *Maiasaura*   2 - C *Ankylosaurus*
3 - E *Spinosaurus*   4 - B *Therizinosaurus*
5 - A *Tyrannosaurus*   6 - D *Yangchuanosaurus*

MAZES   48–49

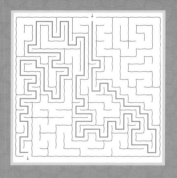 

SPOT THE DIFFERENCE   50–51

QUIZ WHIZ

1. b – Bananas
2. a – *Tsintaosaurus*
3. c – Laid eggs
4. b – Bony lump
5. a – 3 feet (1 m)

6. b – Diamonds
7. c – They were blown up.
8. b – Long and thin
9. a – Rotting vegetation
10. b – Armor

WORD JUMBLES

TYRANNOSAURUS
IGUANODON
SPINOSAURUS
MAIASAURA
SHUNOSAURUS

CROSSWORDS

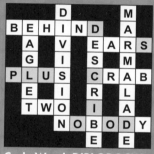

Code Word: *DIPLODOCUS*

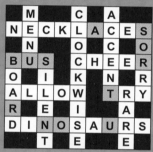

Code Word: *BRONTOSAURUS*

SUDOKUS

4	6	5	1	3	2
1	3	2	4	6	5
6	1	3	5	2	4
2	5	4	6	1	3
3	4	1	2	5	6
5	2	6	3	4	1

5	3	2	6	1	4
1	4	6	2	5	3
3	2	1	4	6	5
4	6	5	3	2	1
6	1	4	5	3	2
2	5	3	1	4	6

4	5	1	2	6	3
2	3	6	4	1	5
3	1	4	6	5	2
5	6	2	3	4	1
1	4	3	5	2	6
6	2	5	1	3	4

SOLUTIONS

WORD SEARCHES
60-61

MATCH GAME
62-63

1 - E *Diplodocus*

2 - F *Alamosaurus*

3 - D *Apatosaurus*

4 - B *Saltasaurus*

5 - C *Argentinosaurus*

6 - A *Mamenchisaurus*

MAZES
64-65

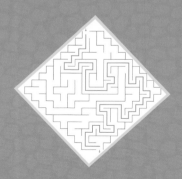

SPOT THE DIFFERENCE

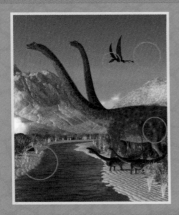

QUIZ WHIZ

1. b – *Apatosaurus*
2. a – Two chicken eggs
3. b – 80 tons (70 t)
4. c – Argentina
5. b – 24 feet (7 m)

6. a – Morocco
7. c – Builders
8. b – Fur
9. c – Toes
10. a – Museums

WORD JUMBLES

DIPLODOCUS
BRONTOSAURUS

BRACHIOSAURUS
MAMENCHISAURUS

ARGENTINOSAURUS

CROSSWORDS

Code Word: PTERODACTYL

Code Word: ICHTHYOSAURS

SOLUTIONS

SUDOKUS 74-75

3	5	6	2	4	1
4	2	1	5	3	6
1	4	5	3	6	2
2	6	3	1	5	4
5	1	4	6	2	3
6	3	2	4	1	5

4	6	3	2	5	1
2	5	1	3	6	4
3	4	6	1	2	5
5	1	2	6	4	3
6	3	4	5	1	2
1	2	5	4	3	6

4	5	1	3	6	2
3	6	2	1	4	5
5	1	6	2	3	4
2	4	3	6	5	1
6	2	4	5	1	3
1	3	5	4	2	6

WORD SEARCHES 76-77

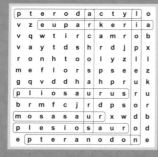

MAZES 78-79

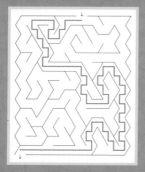

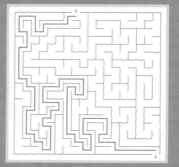